KATE CHAPMAN
ADOBE BUILDER IN 1930s SANTA FE

KATE CHAPMAN

ADOBE BUILDER IN 1930s SANTA FE

Catherine Colby

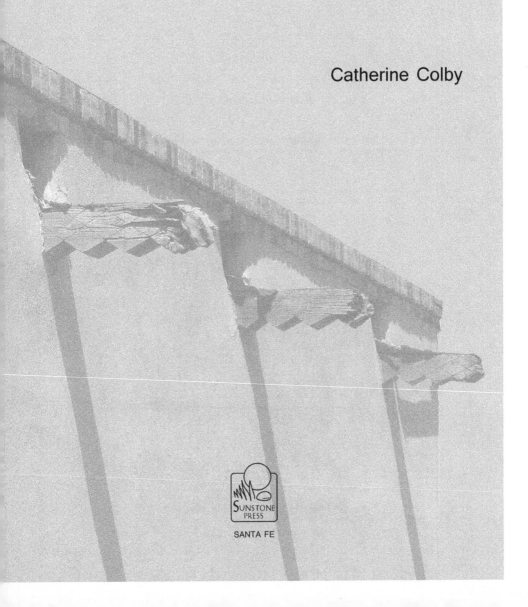

SUNSTONE
PRESS

SANTA FE

Sunstone books may be purchased for educational, business, or sales promotional use.
For information please write: Special Markets Department, Sunstone Press,
P.O. Box 2321, Santa Fe, New Mexico 87504-2321.

Book and Cover design › Vicki Ahl
Body typeface › Adobe Hebrew
Printed on acid-free paper
∞

Library of Congress Cataloging-in-Publication Data

Colby, Catherine, 1944-
  Kate Chapman : adobe builder in 1930s Santa Fe / by Catherine Colby.
     pages cm
  Includes bibliographical references and index.
  ISBN 978-0-86534-912-4 (softcover : alk. paper)
  1. Chapman, Kate, 1887-1944--Criticism and interpretation. 2. Building, Adobe--New
Mexico--Santa Fe. 3. Santa Fe (N.M.)--Buildings, structures, etc. I. Title.
  NA737.C37C65 2012
  720.92--dc23

                              2012038283

WWW.SUNSTONEPRESS.COM
SUNSTONE PRESS / POST OFFICE BOX 2321 / SANTA FE, NM 87504-2321 /USA
(505) 988-4418 / ORDERS ONLY (800) 243-5644 / FAX (505) 988-1025

Contents

Preface

I n 2003 the director of the Historic Santa Fe Foundation Elaine Bergman enthusiastically "introduced" Kate Chapman to me, speaking of her as if Kate were an old friend. I learned that though Kate had a hand in some well-known historic Santa Fe buildings, such as El Zaguan on Canyon Road, she remained relatively unknown. I learned that she and artist Dorothy N. Stewart were adventurous characters who traveled around the southwest in a 1920s precursor to a van that resembled a pioneer covered wagon. I was soon convinced that others would like to "meet" her too.

One glimpse of the booklet that she and Dorothy N. Stewart produced entitled *Adobe Notes or How to Keep the Weather Out With Just Plain Mud* reinforced the need for a book about Kate Chapman's contribution to Santa Fe historic preservation and architecture. I was convinced the small publication deserved to be printed again, incorporated into the book project I was ready to undertake. Kate's booklet combines practical tips on adobe techniques and an authoritative stance about styles with a folksy charm. The Spanish Colonial Arts Society holds the copyright to *Adobe Notes or How to Keep the Weather Out with Just Plain Mud* and graciously gave permission to reprint it within this book.

Kate Chapman did not promote herself or keep records of her work. She did, however, collect photos of some of her building projects. These she pasted into two albums, which ended up with the papers of her more famous husband, Kenneth Chapman. The buildings pictured in the scrapbooks were not identified, and so I set about trying to connect the black and white images taken just after construction in the 1920s and 1930s to buildings existing today.

Kate Chapman's path in Santa Fe is representative of the freedom and acceptance women found here in the 1920s and 1930s. Combining being a mother, poet, adventurer and social activist may have been typical among artists and others in Santa Fe at the time, but to also venture into the predominately male field of adobe construction sets her apart.

Acknowledgements

F or their roles in making this book possible, I am grateful to many people, and principally to Elaine Bergman at the Historic Santa Fe Foundation. I also want to thank Laura Holt, librarian at the School for Advanced Research, and others who helped in many ways: Sarah Burt, Kay Hamilton, Kristin Watson, Jeff Fornaciari, Steve Hughes, Jane Farrar, and Kate Chapman's granddaughter, Peggy Harnisch. I need to acknowledge the prior research of Corinne Sze, Janet Chapman, Karen Barrie and Chris Wilson, and the drawings of architects Donna Quastoff, Dale Zinn and Bob Nestor. I am grateful to Bill Field and Robin Farwell Gavin at the Spanish Colonial Arts Museum for facilitating the reprinting of *Adobe Notes or How to Keep Out the Weather with Just Plain Mud*.

1

Kate Muller Chapman's Early Years in Santa Fe, 1910–1917

A t the age of twenty-four Katherine Antonia Muller left her home in Philadelphia and arrived in Santa Fe for the second time in her life. The first time, in 1899, she temporarily moved with her family because of her brother's poor health. At that time, Kate attended the Loretto Academy, and when she returned to Philadelphia went to a convent school before studying at the Pennsylvania Art School for two years. By 1910 the independent young woman was ready to return for a summer stay in Santa Fe.

Kate Muller signed up for the summer archaeology program offered in Santa Fe by the combined Museum of New Mexico and School of American Archaeology. Just established by the Territorial Legislature the year before, the new institutions under the direction of Edgar L. Hewett were housed in the old Palace of the Governors on the Plaza. The school charged a registration fee of five dollars, which admitted students to all the courses offered, except sketching classes. Students were required to share the living expenses during fieldwork sessions.[1]

Kate attended lectures presented by museum staff members, such as Kenneth Chapman, and took part in the field session on the Pajarito Plateau, now part of Bandelier National Monument. Edgar L. Hewett hired men from San Ildefonso Pueblo, including Julian Martinez, husband of the famed potter, Maria, to help with the archaeological excavations at the summer field sessions.[2] Kate's friendship with Julian is evident in a photo taken in 1910 or 1911.

Kate Muller (later Chapman) with Julian Martinez during an archaeological field session on the Pajarito Plateau c.a. 1910. Photograph courtesy of School for Advanced Research (SAR ACo2_818.a).

Kate Muller's interest in archaeology and later volunteer work with exhibits at the museum in Santa Fe brought her into contact not only with her future husband but also into the midst of events that would soon change the national reputation of the city. Improving Santa Fe's economy became crucial after the railroad arrived in New Mexico in 1888. The faster mode of transportation caused the demise of the trade over the Santa Fe Trail and therefore ended Santa Fe's position as a thriving commercial center. The main line of the railroad bypassed the Territorial capital, and only a spur line was built from Lamy to Santa Fe. As a result, Albuquerque experienced rapid growth while the capital declined.

To many residents of Santa Fe, in the 1880s progress and economic improvement meant achieving statehood and believing New Mexico should resemble the existing states. In terms of architecture, this meant adopting various architectural styles that were popular in the Midwest and eastern United States. Thus, some Santa Feans disparaged adobe as a backward building material. The railroad facilitated the trend away from the traditional adobe architecture by transporting new building materials more cheaply than ever before. Everything from large Queen Anne houses and Italianate commercial buildings to rows of brick bungalows appeared in Santa Fe by the time Kate Muller arrived in 1910.

By participating in the events of the museum and school, Kate Muller found herself in the center of Hewett's staff members and other civic-minded newcomers who admired the disappearing adobe architecture. They saw this regional and unique architecture as the key, not the hindrance, to progress and economic success. The major reorientation of Santa Fe's architecture, back to adobe, began among the small group led by the director and staff of the museum. The group urged citizens to value regional adobe architectural traditions and to cease building in the "American" styles.

Kate's arrival in Santa Fe coincided exactly with these new efforts to revive elements of traditional architecture. She immersed herself in the movement to such an extent that when distinguished architectural historian and professor at University of New Mexico, Bainbridge Bunting, later described Santa Fe in this period, he counted Kate Chapman among those on the ". . . crusade to safeguard the heritage of the Southwest."[3] Though the museum staff members and other promoters of a unique image for Santa Fe spoke of preservation and named it Santa Fe style, they went far beyond simply maintaining the existing adobe buildings in Santa Fe. In reality, what they proposed was a new revival style incorporating many qualities that were not present within Santa Fe, but mainly outside the city, particularly in the nearby pueblos.

Pueblo residents had gradually adopted some of the building features of the Spanish tradition into their room block architecture after the Spaniards arrived in New Mexico in the seventeenth century. Spanish features such as porticos, carving on lintels and corbels, and *hornos,* the Spanish beehive shaped outdoor ovens, gradually appeared in pueblos. Though both the Pueblo and Spanish building traditions combined the modular unit of a single room with the maximum dimension being what logs could span, their end results differed greatly in form and scale. The major and very important distinction between the architecture existing in Santa Fe and in some pueblos was in the massing. The large terraced pueblo blocks rose from three to five stories in some cases, and the roofs of the lower rooms were used as outdoor space for the tasks of daily living. This pattern did not characterize every pueblo, and some had more linear arrangements of rooms and buildings. However, historic photographs illustrate that houses in Santa Fe were predominantly one story. The terraced multi-story pueblo massing was uncommon in Santa Fe before the group at the museum imposed the revival architecture on the city in the early twentieth century.

Within the group that was studying regional architecture and recommending what they called the "New-Old Santa Fe Style," professional architects were conspicuously absent. The licensing of architects and regulation of the profession was only introduced in the New Mexico Territorial Council in 1901, and no formal act was passed until 1931. There were two architects associated with the burgeoning revival style, but neither Isaac Hamilton Rapp nor William Templeton Johnson were involved in the process of defining the exact assemblage of architectural elements conceived in 1912 by the museum staff members. Isaac Hamilton Rapp's Gross Kelly Warehouse and Fine Arts Museum exemplified the local revival style, but Rapp was just as skilled at designing in the Romanesque Revival or Classical Revival styles. Architect William Templeton Johnson produced no buildings in Santa Fe, but argued in writing for the importance of preserving Santa Fe's historic character and served on the city planning board.

Rather than architects, anthropologists and artists on the original museum staff were engaged in researching, defining and promoting the new architectural image for Santa Fe. The principal players were Jesse L. Nusbaum, head of the Architectural Reconstruction and Photography Departments and Sylvanus G. Morley, whose niche was the Archaeology of Central America Department.[4] Along with Nusbaum and Morley, the third man to exert a strong influence on the codification and promotion of the style was artist Carlos Vierra, who joined the staff of the museum and school in 1912. Of the three most influential in the arena of architecture, Vierra was the only one who actually wrote disparagingly of architects' ability to influence such a major shift in their own profession. In a 1918 issue of the periodical, *Art and Archaeology*, Vierra wrote:

> It is an error natural to architects who, under the influence of conventional training, are inclined to see everything through the cold and formal medium of mathematical precision and symmetry. . . . The architect who is to be successful with it need not ignore mathematics, but he must not allow mathematical precision to interfere where it has no place, and where its absence is essential. It is in reality a freehand architecture, with the living quality of a sculptor's work.[5]

Carlos Vierra emphasized the sculptural qualities of mission church towers and the terraced, asymmetrical, multi-story architecture in the pueblos over the primarily one-story, linear Spanish architecture still existing in many parts of Santa Fe. Vierra objected to the fired red bricks introduced as protective cornices on adobe parapets. He disparaged all the "American" architectural features that became popular in Santa Fe after New Mexico became a U.S. Territory in 1846. For Vierra, the new materials constituted a contamination of the adobe architecture of the previous Spanish and Mexican periods. The new features derived from a simplified Greek revival style, and one completely superficial shape became emblematic of the makeovers of preexisting adobe buildings. This was the element at the head of windows and doors: the thin applied trim expressing a reference to a Greek temple pediment. Less superficially, a new symmetry and verticality of proportion was introduced into existing and new adobe buildings after New Mexico became a U.S. Territory. Traditionally, door and window openings were set back in their openings, usually bull-nosed at the exterior, and often had a heavy exposed wood lintel. During what is known as the Territorial period, window openings increased in size and verticality, were surrounded by wood trim, and doors were often set between tall sidelights.

Territorial features and proportions appeared in the Palace of the Governors as well as residences. Museum staff member Jesse Nusbaum supervised repairs and alterations to the Palace building for Edgar Hewett. The stated intent was to remove all changes made by the Americans, in order to "restore" the palace to its pre-1846 appearance.[6] The front of the palace had been altered twice in the late nineteenth century. A photograph of the Corpus Christi procession in front of the palace in the early 1870s shows that the mud-roofed adobe palace had a simple *portal* with a plain milled fascia supported on tapering, thin square columns and small caps of mitered wood molding. By the 1880s the portal stepped forward slightly at intervals. A wood balustrade with a railing of cutout wood, and finials on the posts above each porch column added a more elaborate decorative aspect. A standing-seam metal roof with brick chimneys had already replaced the former mud roof of the building by the turn of the twentieth century. These changes had represented modernization when the prevalent ideas of progress meant looking eastward.

In the opinion of Jesse Nusbaum, the light, square columns looked spindly. He sought a much more massive front to the building. However, with the bias and romanticism of a newcomer to Santa Fe, Nusbaum perhaps did not recognize his exaggeration and conjecture of what the building had been. While claiming his new *portal* was based on a corbel found embedded in a wall at the Palace, he designed a wood *portal* structure that was larger in scale. Similarly, the solid masses at the ends of the portal, he claimed, were based on the only documentation of the south side of the building before 1867, the map drawn by José de Urrutia. The map shows the footprint of solid masses at the east and west ends of the building, but they may have been enclosed, and their serving as open passages is conjectural. Nusbaum added the features representative of a romantic view of the past that was popular in the twentieth century; yet Nusbaum's *portal* will probably survive for centuries as supposed representative of the "ancient" history of Santa Fe.

On the interior of the Palace of the Governors the so-called restoration work included demolishing some interior walls, cutting new door openings in adobe walls, removing wood casings at doors, and adding new fireplaces. This major project went on between 1909 and 1912, the period when Kate Muller involved herself at the museum. Part of the work included interior changes necessary to create larger spaces for exhibits, including a "New-Old Santa Fe Style Exhibit" intended to explain the new revival style, and to show residents example buildings.

Museum staff members included architects' drawings in the exhibit, though two of the buildings depicted were not in Santa Fe, but in Lamy, New Mexico and in Colorado. The creators of the museum exhibit regarded the railroad hotel in Lamy as the best contemporary example of the new style they imagined for Santa Fe.[7] Architect Louis Curtiss of Kansas City had designed the hotel named El Ortiz for the Atchison Topeka and Santa Fe Railway in 1909. However, in addition to local features like *viga* ends projecting beyond the exterior wall plane and carved corbels under heavy wood beams, Curtiss also combined a variety of design elements in his hotel, including California Mission revival style motifs.

The second architectural drawing in the 1912 Exhibition was a rendering by Isaac Hamilton Rapp showing a building with the features the museum staff members were promoting. Ironically, in 1908 when the architects in the Rapp Brothers firm had first expressed ideas similar to those brewing in Santa Fe in 1910, it was not even in New Mexico. More importantly, the architects were not searching for a new direction or style for building in Santa Fe or anywhere else. The building chosen for the exhibition derived simply from the Rapp firm's client specifying that the new Colorado Supply Company Warehouse be based on a specific Pueblo Mission. The warehouse was built in Morley, Colorado, and it resembled the San Esteban del Rey Mission church at Acoma.[8]

Among the exhibits was also a full-scale example of the kind of *portal* considered appropriate for future buildings in Santa Fe. The young Kate Muller loaned the museum the full-sized *portal* structure for the exhibit. She would later incorporate it into the remodeling of the apartment where she was living at the Boyle house, work she accomplished in exchange for rent.[9] Installing the portal on the east side of the house called for alterations including adding an adobe masonry parapet. Thus, between 1910 and 1912 Kate found herself in a position to simultaneously learn the tenets of the revival architectural movement from her colleagues at the museum, witness firsthand how the adobe Palace of the Governors was constructed and being altered, and to venture into her own adobe construction. These three streams that converged for Kate by 1912 probably served as preparation for her later accomplishments in adobe architecture.

Kate Muller (later Chapman) at the *portal* she added to the east side of her apartment at the Boyle house. Photograph courtesy of School for Advanced Research (SAR AC02_743.ct).

The *portal* in 2008.

Museum staff member Kenneth Chapman also contributed to the "New-Old Santa Fe Style Exhibit" in 1912. Officially Kenneth Chapman served as both Secretary and as the sole member of the Illustrating Department at the museum. While primarily occupied with his work on Pueblo pottery and carrying out the numerous duties of his job, Kenneth Chapman also played a role in the definition of Santa Fe style. Sylvanus Morley and Kenneth Chapman both had contributed their input about the proportions and details of Jesse Nusbaum's new *portal* at the Palace of the Governors.[10] Two years before he would marry Kate, Kenneth Chapman demonstrated his knowledge of the concepts of the new style by entering the contest sponsored by the Chamber of Commerce for the best drawing of a hypothetical Santa Fe Style house. Kenneth Chapman won first prize, and Carlos Vierra won second place. Kenneth Chapman also produced renderings of a hypothetical hotel, post office and of the east side of the Palace combined with the building north of it, but in terms of the new architecture his work was primarily as illustrator.

Of the museum staff members, Carlos Vierra went to the greatest lengths to illustrate the new revival style by actually building an example as his home. The house had two stories with a complex, terrace-like irregular massing of forms. The building featured rounded corners, inset porches with oversized round wood posts, and corbels and beams beneath adobe parapets. *Viga* ends projected through walls, and exposed heavy wood lintels extended beyond the sides of window openings. An eroding adobe wall enclosed the yard and rose to step up over the exposed lintel of a tall, door-sized gate.

At the same time Carlos Vierra, Kate Muller, and Kenneth Chapman were making their individual forays into architecture, they all used their drawing skills to document rock art in Frijoles Canyon on the Pajarito Plateau. In 1915 the three made over one hundred sketches in the cliff dwellings.[11] Kenneth and Kate were working together both in Santa Fe and in Frijoles Canyon when they announced their plans for a September wedding. After the event, which took place at St. Francis Cathedral, Kate and Kenneth spent their honeymoon exploring cliff dwellings at Puye and Santa Clara. The following year the Chapmans were back at Frijoles Canyon working for the museum, camping out even during Kate's pregnancy. In 1917 the couple bought an adobe house located southeast of downtown on the road then called East Manhattan and now known as Acequia Madre. The Chapman property was an approximately six-acre parcel of land north of the acequia or irrigation ditch. The area was rural, having expanses of fields and orchards with small adobe houses clustered close to the few dirt roads.

The area where the Chapmans bought their first house in 1917 was rural and sparsely settled. The Chapmans lived on the property shown shaded gray at the upper right. It would later become Plaza Balentine. The two other shaded properties south of Acequia Madre are those Kate purchased later. Her rehabilitations there are described in Chapter 2. (Based on a detail of the Official Map of Santa Fe drawn by N.L. King in 1912.)

According to deeds, the grounds of the Chapman property north of the Acequia Madre included an orchard, fields, and a chicken house. At the north were a garage, well and water tower consisting of a metal tank on a timber base. A picket fence enclosed the front yard of the house that contained a small wood pyramidal-roofed well house. The Chapmans lived in this location for close to twenty years and raised their family there; son Frank and daughter Helen were born in 1917 and 1919. On the back of one of her photographs of their house Kate wrote,

> "This is our house. Out back, you can see the chicken house—we have dozens of eggs . . . for our winter use, and

over 300 glasses and jars of fruits of different sorts. Aren't
we thrifty?"[12]

A picket fence enclosed the front yard of the home the Chapmans bought on Acequia Madre.
Photograph c.a.1917 courtesy of School for Advanced Research (SAR AC02_805.e).

Kate and Kenneth Chapman with their daughter Helen at the east end of the house at 615 Acequia
Madre. Photograph courtesy Museum of New Mexico (# 028144).

High adobe walls were later added at the south and east sides of the house on Acequia Madre. Photograph courtesy of School for Advanced Research (SAR ACo2_16.bl).

By 2008 the well structure was demolished and the portal enclosed. Henry J. Hughes, who moved to Plaza Balentine in 1944, added the stone wing wall and wood sign.[13] Around 1920 Kate took the initiative to embark on the design and construction of two new houses on their land. The first two were located northeast of their own house, and the compound became known as Plaza Balentine by 1923.

2

Plaza Balentine

Northeast of the Chapman home on Acequia Madre, Kate Chapman designed the first two houses of what would become the residential compound known as Plaza Balentine. She directed a crew of workers to build the houses facing a new private driveway leading northward from East Manhattan. The name of her compound, Plaza Balentine, is mentioned in deeds beginning as early as 1923, but exactly when or how the name Balentine originated is not recorded. Naming residential compounds *Plaza* was common in early twentieth century Santa Fe, as newcomers freely adapted the Spanish word. In eighteenth and nineteenth century New Mexico, a *plaza* was a settlement comprised of adjoining houses organized around a central open space. The word *plaza* came to also indicate the enclosed area itself. The houses in the Santa Fe compounds of the 1920s, such as Plaza Chamisal and the Webster Compound on Garcia Street may not follow the exact centralized pattern, but houses were oriented within the lot, grouped away from the street. Placement of the houses fostered interaction among residents by omitting individual yards or high fences to separate each house.

Kate may have derived the name of her compound from that of the former owner of the property. An L-shaped adobe house is shown on the property in the Official Map of Santa Fe prepared in 1912 by N.L. King, chief draftsman with the United States Land Office. The probable builder of that house, Valentine Herbert, sold the six-acre property north of the

Acequia Madre to Robert L. Douthitt in 1901. However, the buyer did not live there, and instead, Rosario Martinez de Herbert (Valentine's ex-wife) and her daughter were still living in the house in 1910. Valentine Herbert was a carpenter, who emigrated from Bavaria to the U.S. and married the New Mexico native, Rosario Martinez.[1]

The first two houses Kate designed and built on Plaza Balentine were almost 100 feet north of the street and the *acequia*. Kate's first house excluded any of the sculptural, eroded quality of pueblo features urged by artist Carlos Vierra. Rather, it more closely resembles a nineteenth century Santa Fe house, the Roque Lobato house, before Sylvanus Morley bought it in 1912. The Lobato house featured a long central portal flanked by two solid masses. In the second half of the nineteenth century many Santa Fe residents replaced their existing small windows with those having larger areas of glass. Morley removed Lobato's improvements and installed small windows.

The nineteenth century Roque Lobato House in Santa Fe. Photograph by Jesse Nusbaum courtesy Museum of New Mexico (# 010541).

At Kate's first house the centerpiece of the façade is the approximately 15-feet-long *portal*. Kate emulated the traditional building form of the Lobato house and the larger windows as well. She employed traditional round posts and exposed *viga* ends, but departed from the usual details by giving her corbels an angular shape.

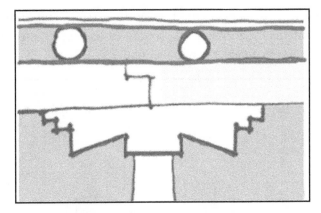

Kate Chapman's angular corbel design.

Kate also framed some vertically proportioned pairs of wood casement windows with milled lumber trim incorporating the pediment shape of the trim at the head, the characteristic feature of the pre-revival Territorial period.

The first house Kate designed and built at Plaza Balentine. Photograph courtesy of School for Advanced Research (SAR AC02_818.16ah).

The design of Kate's second house is a combination of distinct masses joined by a high wall to create a patio. It is an inward-focused composition with an elegant simplicity in the arrangement of forms. The high wall contains the entrance gate, and is set back several feet from the building volumes that flank the patio within.

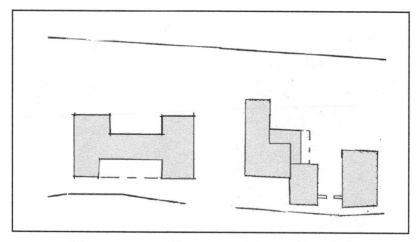

Kate's first house at left was symmetrical, in contrast to the complex irregular assemblage of forms in her second house at right.

Elements expressing the revival style include the heavy exposed lintels over a group of three horizontally grouped casement windows. A simple handmade pair of wood panel gates are placed asymmetrically in the wall, which rises very slightly at each end where it adjoins the building masses. Instead of cutting them off evenly, Kate left the *vigas* extending out at varied lengths. On the south elevation a door opening with a raised sill and flat, high buttress suggest an out-building more than a residence: this part of the building turns away from both the street south of it and the lane west of it. Kate painted the applied milled lumber trim and the small four-panel door in a high contrast light and dark color scheme. The scheme was not a revival style element, but one sometimes seen in architecture of the Territorial Period. Kate's second house at Plaza Balentine had crisp edges at its mud plastered corners and parapets. Even the shallow buttress, so often rendered as a thick sculptural feature in revival style buildings, has a flat lack of exaggeration. In Kate's second house she again displays none of the rounded sculptural quality often associated with the Spanish-Pueblo revival of Santa Fe style.

Kate's second Balentine house displays an elegant arrangement of simple volumes. Photographs courtesy of School for Advanced Research (AC02_16.ai, aj).

The third house Kate built at Plaza Balentine a few years after the first two is adjacent to the road, but oriented towards the lane. Like the second house, it is composed of separate masses, but arranged in a more dispersed and complex composition. The entry to the house is through a small covered passage. Its end wall contained an arched opening through which one could glimpse a separate part of the building through a wood picket gate. The beam of the passage is supported on Kate's angular corbels, and the scuppers draining the roof of the north mass are detailed with a zigzag motif at the bottom edges. The single and grouped casement windows have Territorial style applied wood trim. The pediment heads are ornamented with dentils under the cap piece, and extend beyond the trim at the sides of the windows.

Coincidentally, by 1930 Kate's first building was occupied by the man who may have unknowingly affected her decision to start designing and building, Jesse Nusbaum. By then, he had become Acting Director of the School for American Research and lived at Plaza Balentine with his wife Eileen and son Deric. The remaining two houses in Plaza Balentine were not finished until 1936–1937. An outbuilding was converted into another house. Much later, the pre-existing garage was converted to part of a residence, but the water tower and galvanized tank remained for more than fifty years longer. Over the years, Kate's second and third houses at Plaza Balentine have been greatly altered, making Kate's photos particularly important as indications of her design ability. They also demonstrate her originality in not always following the tenets of the newly sanctioned Santa Fe style.

The entrance to the third house at Plaza Balentine with Kate's distinctive angular corbels and zigzag edges at the bottom of the canales. Photograph courtesy of School for Advanced Research (SAR AC02_81816.f).

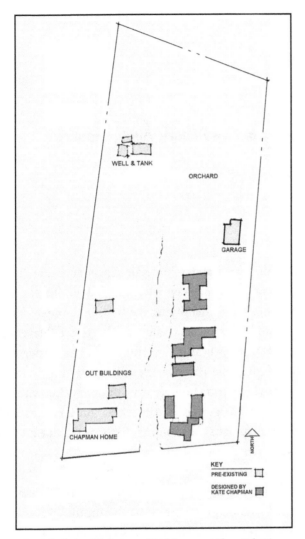

Spatial relationship between Kate's houses at Plaza Balentine.

3

Rehabilitations of Five Historic Adobe Houses

D uring the 1920s and 1930s Kate Chapman rehabilitated several
eighteenth and nineteenth century adobe houses in Santa Fe.
The names now identifying the houses commemorate the early
owner/builders and later owners, such as the Garcia-Stevenson House,
Juan José Prada House, Delgado-Hare House, and the Borrego House. The
exception to including the name of the original builder along with later
owner is the James L. Johnson house, more commonly known as El Zaguan.
These buildings are recognized as important in Santa Fe's architectural
history, but Kate Chapman's contributions to them are little known. Though
she acted as designer and construction manager, Kate Chapman did not
promote herself as either.

When Kate began her work in the early 1920s, many Santa Fe
buildings lacked indoor plumbing, though running water had become
available to some residents after the construction of Two-Mile Dam in
1893. Kate altered the interiors of nineteenth century houses to introduce
bathrooms, and also designed additions. She repeatedly demonstrated her
skill and sensitivity while carrying out alterations by respecting the innate
character of a historic building. Even when the square footage of her
additions was larger than the original house, the additions were carefully
positioned to avoid overwhelming the old house. At the same time, she
did no slavish copying of details. She introduced her own idiosyncratic

style, sometimes using angular corbels, doors with angled tops, arched windows and rectangular fireplace openings of her own devising. She also applied high contrast paint colors on doors or shutters. Many of Kate's design features are not those stipulated for Santa Fe Style, and the eroded sculptural quality promoted by Carlos Vierra is not a hallmark of her work.

In the houses Kate updated, the existing heating sources were more often wood stoves than fireplaces. Long-time New Mexican residents appreciated the greater efficiency the stoves provided. But the early twentieth century newcomers loved the romance of the fireplace, and usually added new fireplaces in historic houses that did not contain them. Kate's friend and client, Margretta Dietrich, admired Kate for bringing Pueblo women into Santa Fe to introduce new fireplaces into the old Spanish-built houses she was remodeling. But before the Spanish conquest, the Pueblo Indians did not have corner fireplaces. They used open central floor hearths and only under Spanish influence gradually adopted the Spanish corner fireplace called a *fogon* in Spanish. When the Pueblo Indians introduced the Spanish fireplaces into their rooms, they did make adjustments, often adding chimney pots and improvising the shape of the opening in order to fit their traditional granite griddles over the fire.[1] The misnomer, kiva fireplace, has perhaps added to the misattribution of the corner fireplaces as originating in the pueblos.

At the time Kate embarked on remodeling historic houses, she was raising two young children and designing/building the new Plaza Balentine houses on the land she and her husband had purchased in 1917. Only three years after moving into their house at 615 Acequia Madre, when the Chapman's son Frank was three and daughter Helen was only one year old, Kate began purchasing nearby land southwest of Plaza Balentine. In the early 1920s members of the Garcia and Delgado families sold their properties on the other side of Acequia Madre to Kate. She designed and built additions to the two old houses at the northern ends of the Garcia and Delgado properties, and subdivided and sold the southern portions of the two lots. Thus, developer may be added to Kate's designer and construction manager titles.

Garcia-Stevenson House, Acequia Madre

Southwest of the Chapman house and Plaza Balentine were the houses, corrals and fields where the Garcia family had lived since the mid-nineteenth century. Rafael Garcia bought the land from Antonio Maria Archuleta in 1848, and later followed the locally common practice of bequeathing individual rooms of his house to each child. When Santa Fe's houses were recorded on the Official Map produced in 1912 by the chief draftsman in the U.S. Land Office, the Garcia's house was a series of contiguous spaces that had been added over the years. It consisted of a double file of rooms at the east and an L-shaped portion at the west. By 1920, when Kate purchased the east side of the rectangular portion, it was owned by Magdalena de Garcia. The next year Kate was able to buy the contiguous row of rooms attached at the west from Nicolas M. Garcia. The L-shaped part of the house remained a separate property, later to become the location of another residential compound named Placita Rafaela.

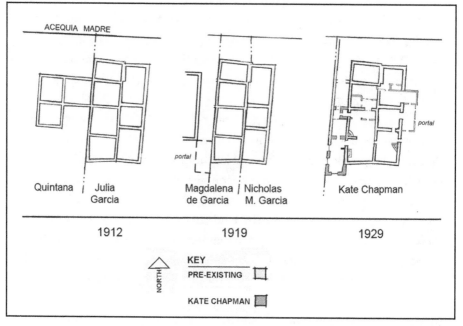

Evolution of the Garcia house between 1912 and 1929. The 1929 configuration reflects Kate's rehabilitation and additions.

In 1920 the west property line was immediately adjacent to the house. Five years later it was moved several feet westward the width of the former southwest porch. Kate designed and constructed a new entry in the narrow passage this created, and enclosed the preexisting porch with windows and the unique angular-shaped door. At the entry passage she employed the same geometrically cut corbels as she used at Plaza Balentine.

A group including Katherine Stinson Otero standing in front of the entry at the west side of the house when owned by playwright and novelist Philip Edward Stevenson, known as Ted, and his wife Janet. Photograph courtesy of Katherine Stinson Pictorial Collection, Center for Southwest Research (PICT 000-506).

Kate's remodeling of the Garcia-Stevenson house also included breaking through the party wall between the two sets of parallel rooms in two places to recombine them into a single house. She inserted bathrooms and fireplaces. Kate demolished parts of interior walls to enlarge some spaces, and cut a new opening in an exterior wall to extend one room eastward. The new entrance into the room was under a simple *portal.*

Delgado-Hare House

Kate purchased the property east of the Garcia House in 1924 from
Ildeberto Delgado. His father Francisco Delgado had bought it from the
Vigil family in 1911. When the property was depicted in the Official Map
of 1912, the house was L-shaped, but by the 1920s only a rectangular part of
it remained. Delgado Street was not yet extended south of Acequia Madre
to create Delgado Lane. In 1924 Kate set to work designing and building
additions on the south side of the existing house and inserting partition
walls in the existing rectangular building to provide circulation, bathrooms,
and closets. Three years after finishing the work on the house, Kate sold it
to painter and philanthropist, Elizabeth Sage Goodwin Hare. Jane Farrar,
Hare's daughter, knew the house as a child and owns it now. Farrar still
appreciates the layout and light of Kate's alterations and additions.

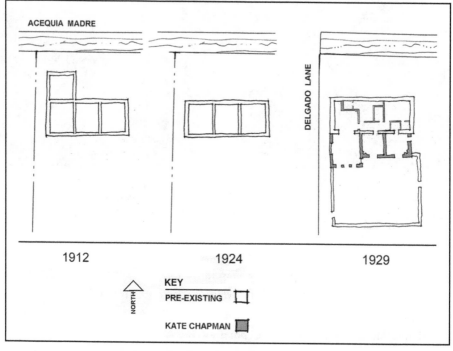

Evolution of the Delgado house between 1912 and 1929, showing Kate's rehabilitation and
additions.

Kate added a living room and bedrooms and, in a departure from the "rules" of the revival style and in contrast to the openings in the existing house, introduced symmetrically placed arched openings for windows and arched glazing panels in doors. The small corner fireplaces in the bedrooms have rectangular openings and shallow plastered hearths raised only a few inches above the floor. On the living room addition, the door and flanking windows are set symmetrically in the wall.

Living room portion of the south addition to the Delgado House after construction.
Photograph courtesy of School for Advanced Research (SAR AC02_16.i).

Prada House, Canyon Road

Kate's success with building projects led fellow Philadelphia native and political activist Margretta Dietrich to entrust Kate with finding and rehabilitating a nineteenth century adobe house for her on Canyon Road. In 1927 Kate showed Dietrich a house at 519 Canyon Road and introduced her to Miguel Gorman, the owner who was ready to sell. She then facilitated the purchase while Dietrich temporarily returned to the east, according to Dietrich's *New Mexico Recollections Part II.* When Margretta Dietrich purchased the house, now known as the Juan José Prada house, the building comprised only four rooms, which had been part of the Prada family property before Miguel Gorman acquired it. Dietrich moved into the east side in 1928, but did not purchase the adjacent lot until the mid-1930s.

Kate Chapman's involvement in enlarging the house Dietrich bought lasted over a decade, beginning with the basic upgrading to the four rooms before Dietrich permanently moved to Santa Fe. Kate supervised bringing city water to the house, installing plumbing and electrical systems, and replacing the dirt roof. The portal, passage and additional rooms Kate designed north of the existing house produced a cohesive whole, continuing the existing Territorial detailing such as the brick coping and the vertical proportions of the double hung windows.

Margretta Dietrich purchased the adjoining property west of hers in 1937, and Kate then designed rooms to replace the deteriorated ruins that remained there. For the west additions, Dietrich noted in her memoirs that she wanted "really handsome ceilings." She had a set of *vigas* brought from the deserted village of Cow Springs near Tucumcari, New Mexico. Horses had to drag the logs to the closest road. Dietrich, like many of her contemporaries, delighted in finding wood structural elements and doors from ruined buildings to incorporate into their projects in Santa Fe. She also salvaged a door from a downtown Santa Fe building to use as her garden gate. (The door previously led to a butcher shop in a row of adobes on San Francisco Street, buildings that were demolished to make way for construction of the Lensic Theatre in the late 1920s.) Dietrich's sister

Dorothy Stewart painted Mexico-influenced murals at the house where she and her sister lived. Also according to Dietrich's memoirs, when she wished to add fireplaces in existing rooms or new rooms, she relied on Kate to find her women from Tesuque and Cochiti Pueblos to build them.

The design of additions and changes to the Prada house illustrates Kate Chapman's skill in respecting the details and the general architectural character of a historic house. Her addition was not in the new Santa Fe Style. Instead, she sensitively set the long Territorial Revival style porch a distance back from the east side of the existing rectangular building in a way that creates a smooth transition between old and new. Together they form a cohesive whole.

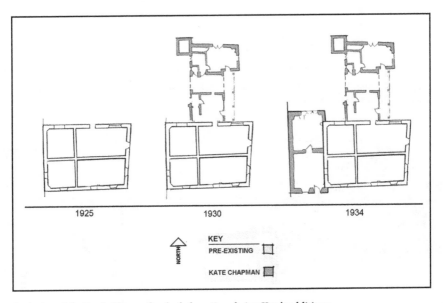

Evolution of the Prada House; the shaded portions being Kate's additions. (Based on drawing by Bob Nestor.)

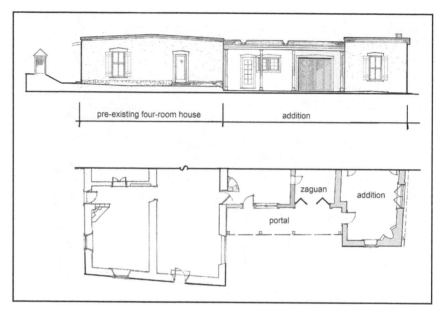

Detail of plan and elevation of Kate's addition on the east side of the Prada house.
(Based on drawings by Bob Nestor.)

South side of the Prada house with the original part at left and Kate Chapman's addition at the
right. Below are two photos of the east side of the house. Photograph courtesy of School for
Advanced Research (SAR AC02_16.t,u,v,z).

El Zaguan and the New Compound

Margretta Dietrich had purchased the property east of the Prada House in 1924, and Kate Chapman carried out many alterations there between 1925 and 1939. Kate introduced a number of small modifications in the main house while she preserved the essential New Mexico Territorial era character that the house developed when owned by James L. Johnson between 1854 and 1900. The very long building Margretta Dietrich soon named El Zaguan continues to present an impressive image along Canyon Road, and is complemented by the mature pair of horse chestnut trees and the picket fenced flower garden at the west.

The facade of El Zaguan maintains its Territorial era character in the twenty-first century. Kate raised the entry wall into the patio and introduced the exposed lintel and full height wood panel gates.

Kate brought the entry patio wall from its previous height of about three feet up to the height that would accommodate a wood lintel and a pair of wood panel gates. The lattice enclosure is still present at the end of the west *portal*. A similar lattice screen that formerly enclosed the south-facing *portal* within the entrance patio was replaced with wood panel folding doors. New brick pavers in an irregular herringbone pattern replaced the old wood flooring. Kate updated the main house to create apartments for Margretta Dietrich, who used the building as an inn, a girls' school, and then as rental apartments.

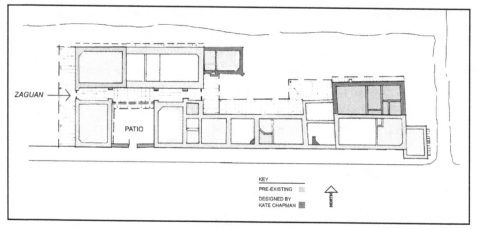

ZAGUAN

PATIO

KEY
PRE-EXISTING
DESIGNED BY
KATE CHAPMAN

NORTH

Floor plan diagram of El Zaguan where Kate added fireplaces and bathrooms as well as additional rooms. (Based on drawing by Dale Zinn.)

Kate Chapman's major impact at El Zaguan took place on the remainder of the large property, where the land had formerly supported subsistence agriculture. When purchased, the land north of the house sloped gently down to an alfalfa field, barn and chicken house. The Canyon Road Community Ditch flowed west behind the main house, turned south in front of the west *portal* until reaching the south edge of the garden, where it turned west and continued down Canyon Road. The ditch irrigated over an acre of farmland behind the house. Kate Chapman transformed the rural site that sloped downhill gradually between Canyon Road and the Santa Fe River into two terraces. Margretta Dietrich asked Kate to modify the existing outbuildings north of the main house to use for residences. Kate divided the site with a stone retaining wall to create two levels with sets of wood steps for access between the upper and lower areas. She then designed the compound of cottages at the lower level centered around an oval landscaped island.

The long passage Margretta Dietrich called the zaguan where Kate had the brick flooring installed.

Kate introduced a new driveway from Canyon Road along the east side of the main house. At the lower level, the driveway loops around the planted oval. On the south side of the landscaped island are two garage/utility buildings Kate nestled into the hillside. The stone retaining wall adjoins the corner of the east garage. Across from these, at the north edge of the site, Kate converted the preexisting outbuildings into cottages. The two-stall garage Kate built at the east side of the compound is divided into two separate spaces by an adobe wall. The roof is supported on *vigas*, which protrude through the west wall along with the *canales*. Kate designed a rustic frame for the garage door opening with exposed log posts at the sides supporting the log lintel above the door opening.

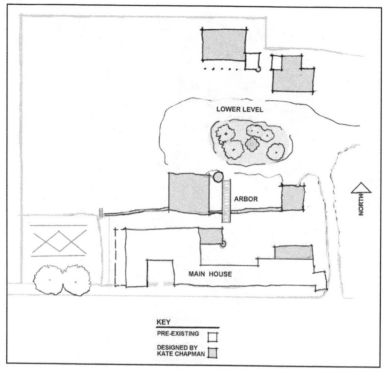

Preexisting house and outbuildings on the site of El Zaguan with Kate's additions after 1925 shaded. (Based on Plat courtesy of the Historic Santa Fe Foundation.)

East garage and adjacent retaining wall at the lower terrace north of El Zaguan. Photograph courtesy of School for Advanced Research (SAR AC02_818.16bc).

At the east end of the main house Kate turned the pedestrian access to the lower level into a major landscape element. Wood steps highlighted with a wood arbor extend about 20 feet in front of and beyond the stairway. This produces a vine-covered passage rising about 15 feet above the lower level. It continues past the steps to create a long, shady passage that is a respite in the summer. The black and white photograph from Kate's photo album shows the stone retaining wall and the wood framing of the arbor soon after completion, with the west garage beyond. Behind the arbor the very tall chimney rose above the boiler room in the garage. Kate used triangular brackets at the corners of the arbor structure, cutting a scalloped edge in the 2-inch-thick lumber and drilling three holes to form a unique feature.

Kate Chapman standing with her new retaining wall, the arbor, horno, and garage/mechanical building at El Zaguan. Photograph courtesy of School for Advanced Research (SAR AC02_818.16b).

The west garage contained stalls for vehicles along with the main house heating system. The north side of the building originally had a window and a pair of doors with glass in the upper part, but these were later replaced with three different pairs of wood garage doors. Each of the present garage doors is constructed with narrow boards, one vertically, one diagonally, and one horizontally. At the north edge of the large site Kate designed an addition on the west side of a small barn, converting it into a cottage. Called cottage #8, it contained a living room, two bedrooms, kitchen and *portal*. Just east of cottage #8 was a small building referred to as a chicken house. Kate initially altered it to serve as a cottage for "the janitor." In 1932 she designed an addition to create another rental cottage. Kate contracted local roofers, plumbers, electricians and painters to implement the construction.

The arbor Kate built at El Zaguan is now covered with lace vine, providing a shady tunnel on hot summer days.

Cottage #8 at El Zaguan, which Kate converted from a small barn. At the right of it is the chicken house before its conversion. Photograph courtesy of School for Advanced Research (SAR AC02_818.16ba).

A group dressed for a theatrical event pose in front of the two cottages north of the main house at El Zaguan. Photograph courtesy of School for Advanced Research (SAR AC02_818.16bb).

Kate emphasized the northeast corner of cottage #8 with a corner fireplace expressed at the exterior. In the background at the right is the addition Kate made to the chicken house, converting it into cottage #9. Here the shutters were painted in a high contrast color scheme, like those at her second house in Plaza Balentine. Windows in cottage #8 were six-light casements in a horizontal configuration with projecting sills and exposed wood lintels. In contrast, the vertically proportioned six-over-six pane wood casement windows of cottage #9 are trimmed with milled wood and include a pediment head and shutters.

Clearly Kate was not aiming for uniformity of style in her compound, and added her own stamp that related neither to Santa Fe Style nor to the Territorial period in New Mexico. Window shutters were excluded from the revival style, but existed on the main house at El Zaguan, and at the Prada house next door. The fence style utilizing unpeeled vertical poles capped with milled lumber appeared in Santa Fe after the turn of the twentieth century and a few examples remain.[2] Were Kate adhering to the revival style, she might have included a thick adobe wall, rather than the fence.

El Zaguan characterizes the changes unfolding in Santa Fe when New Mexico transitioned from a U.S. Territory (1846–1912) to the very different Santa Fe of the 1930s. The main house and picket fence are the "face" along Canyon Road. These features preserve the connections with the Territorial era, but are only part of the story of the property. The whole assemblage exemplifies the trend of American women from cities all over the country relocating to Santa Fe and valuing the historic architecture, while also imposing the imprint of their own backgrounds and worldviews. As a subsistence farm, the animal pens, corrals, fields, and stable supported the family of the merchant James L. Johnson, who came from Maryland in the nineteenth century and married a native of Chihuahua, Mexico. The change in this property is also emblematic of the development of the larger context of the east side of Santa Fe, which passed from a rural to an urban environment.

Borrego House, Canyon Road

The next rehabilitation Kate Chapman completed for Margretta Dietrich won a prize in 1930. Located on Canyon Road east of the Prada House and El Zaguan at the intersection of what is now Camino del Monte Sol, the property is known as the Borrego House. The building once sat on a lot extending all the way south to the Acequia Madre, containing fields and an orchard. But in this case, unlike at El Zaguan, the house had already been separated from much of the land by the time of Dietrich's purchase in 1928. The building has housed a succession of restaurants in the second half of the twentieth century, and a paved parking lot on the east has replaced a former field or orchard.

The striking Territorial era *portal* of the house sits immediately adjacent to the edge of Canyon Road. From the front, like El Zaguan, this building supplies a vivid impression of the architecture of the Territorial period in New Mexico. The façade incorporates the milled lumber and fired bricks that were newly available and the vertical proportions adopted, along with a simplified variant of American Greek Revival architecture. The long *portal* and *sala* or living room behind it were added to the five-room adobe building around 1860.[3]

The identifying feature of the Borrego House is the portal added in about 1860. It exemplifies changes to the city's architecture after the Santa Fe Trail opened in 1846. Historic photographs of Santa Fe show numerous examples of such porches. Photograph by Frederick D. Nichols, 1936. Courtesy of Historic American Building Survey, Library of Congress, Prints and Photograph Division (HABS NM-14).

As at El Zaguan, Kate sensitively altered the Borrego House, staying away from introducing Pueblo-influenced features of the new Santa Fe Style. Her work on the exterior of the building was limited to adding a simple porch roof at the east, a low wall to create a small courtyard on that side, and adding several replacement windows and doors. The majority of her work involved the new interior partitions and new fireplaces, plumbing and replacing the brick and concrete floors in some rooms, while preserving the exterior.

While the street side of the Borrego House represented the progress

of the Territorial era, the rear continued even as late as 1940 to illustrate the
slow transition between the Spanish and Mexican period mud-plastered
adobe architecture to the lime and cement-plastered architecture of the
American period. Before the American occupation in 1846, traditional
adobe houses were usually mud-plastered, had small windows, and rooms
adjoining each other. This linear pattern often created the strong horizontal
quality illustrated here. The color palette was low contrast, essentially the
brown of wood *viga* ends, posts, corbels and beams with the brown of the
mud plaster. The introduction of red brick and white lime wash created a
drastic change in coloration, as well as proportion. Though black and white,
the photographs on the following pages gives a sense of the transition of the
south end of the Borrego House.

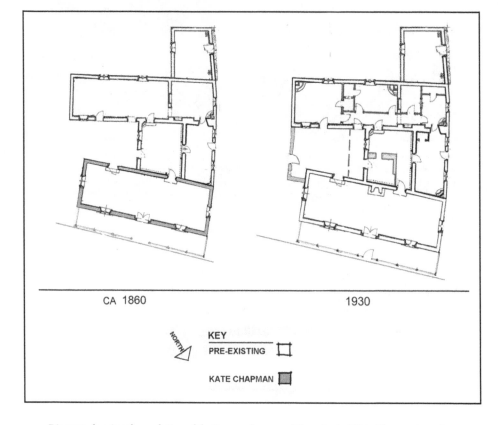

CA 1860   1930

KEY
PRE-EXISTING
KATE CHAPMAN
NORTH

Diagram showing the evolution of the Borrego house and the extent of Kate Chapman's work.

Borrego house from the back (south) showing the lack of Territorial period features. Photograph by Donald W. Dickensheets, 1940. Courtesy of Historic American Building Survey, Library of Congress, Prints and Photograph Division (HABS NM-14).

As at the Garcia House on Acequia Madre, parts of the Borrego House had been bequeathed to various family descendants. The southwest corner room of the house had a separate chain of title, and Margretta Dietrich did not purchase it until 1939, eleven years after she bought the front. The room's exterior was still mud-plastered and in fair condition when photographed in 1940. The associated *coyote* fence of unpeeled vertical poles is another example of the pre-American Santa Fe. This simple fence type originated to protect goats from coyotes, and contrasts strongly with the crisp pickets at the front *portal*.

The west side of the building in 1940 comprised three distinct sections remaining from before the American influences. No architectural relationship exists between the three parts to present a cohesive exterior. One mass contains a large offset door; the next, lower mass has a single, large, almost centered window; and the final mass contains a small door flanked by small double-hung windows. Finally, the latest addition closest to Canyon Road introduces the elements in vogue around 1860, the crisp portal structure and pediment heads at the window, and the vertical proportions in the *portal* and windows.

The west side of the Borrego House photographed in 1940 shows the piecemeal room-by-room fashion additions that were often built in Santa Fe, as well as the contrast between the front of the building and the remaining elevations. Photograph by Donald W. Dickensheets, 1940. Courtesy of Historic American Building Survey, Library of Congress, Prints and Photograph Division (HABS NM-14).

Kate finished her work at the Borrego House in the same year as the first annual architectural competition in Santa Fe, and architect John Gaw Meem was one of the judges. Prizes were $100 each for the best examples of "correct building" constructed between 1928 and 1930. Cyrus McCormick III offered the prize money. He was the grandson of the Cyrus McCormick who invented the mechanical reaper in Illinois in 1831. The younger McCormick spent summers at his ranch in Nambé. He involved himself in local issues and worked with Carlos Vierra and John Gaw Meem on the design of both his grand new house and on rehabilitating the small buildings that he purchased to form Las Acequias ranch.

The competition judges working with McCormick and John Gaw Meem included the physician of Sunmount Sanatorium Dr. Frank E Mera, civic leader H. H. Dorman, and artists Carlos Vierra and Sheldon Parsons. There were three categories of prizes: best rehabilitation, best commercial building, and the best example of a new residence costing between $8,000 and $10,000.[4] The prizewinner in the first category was Kate's project, the Borrego House. The August 30, 1930, issue of *El Pasatiempo*, a publication of the *Santa Fe New Mexican*, displayed photographs of the prize-winning building projects, with the Borrego House at the top of the page. Under it was the caption: "At the top of the page is the house at 724 Canyon Road, owned by Mrs. C. H. Dietrich and designed by Kate Chapman, awarded the prize as the best example of restoration or remodeling done in the period named."

Ten years later John Gaw Meem was serving as the District Officer of the Historic American Buildings Survey (HABS), a federal government program initiated under the Public Works Administration (PWA) to record important buildings in the nation's history. The Borrego House was singled out for the thorough documentation the program provides. With measured drawings, photographs and short text, the significance of the Borrego House architecture was recognized in a national context. The HABS Report by Trent Thomas, based on interviews with José F. Gonzales, Sefarino Alarid and Kate M. Chapman, described the house after Kate's rehabilitation. The house had pine floors, adobe walls, adobe plaster on the interior and exterior; the interior being finished with a thin coat of *yeso*, a whitewash of hand crushed native gypsum applied with lamb's wool pads. The report continued, stating that most of the lumber, the windows, doors and frames were freighted in over the Santa Fe Trail by ox team from Missouri. The mantel of the fireplace in room A (*sala*) was salvaged from one of the officers' buildings of old Fort Marcy in Santa Fe. During an interview with Kate Chapman, she stated that ". . . with the exception of the new frame partitions, new fireplaces, plumbing, brick and cement floors, porch, and *placita* wall, the building is essentially the same as it was prior to the remodeling."

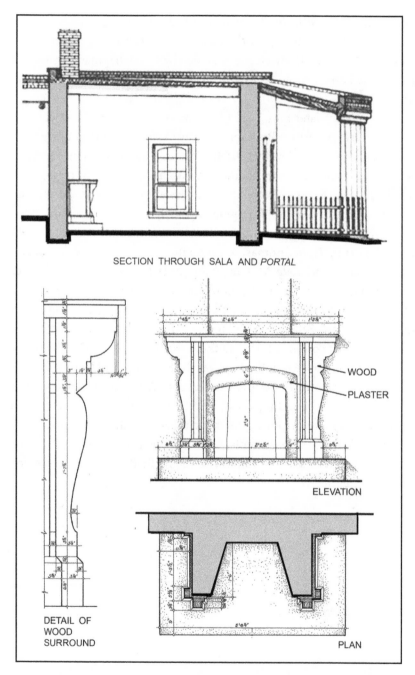

SECTION THROUGH SALA AND *PORTAL*

WOOD

PLASTER

ELEVATION

DETAIL OF
WOOD
SURROUND

PLAN

The fireplace from Fort Marcy shown in relation to the sala and portal, and in three details. (Based on Historic American Buildings Survey Drawings delineated by R. P. McClung.)

4

Adobe Expert and Writer

I n the late 1920s Kate Chapman, collaborating with her close friend and Margretta Dietrich's sister Dorothy Stewart, produced her treatise advising how to build an appropriate adobe house in Santa Fe. Somehow, Kate found time to write it, and in 1930 her *Adobe Notes or How to Keep the Weather Out with Just Plain Mud* was published by Witter Bynner's friend Spud Johnson at his Laughing Horse Press in Taos. Consisting of ten sheets of 9-inch-by-12-inch paper in different pastel colors folded in half and stapled, the little booklet had a cream color paper cover, which was block printed in red ink. The small pages were partially filled with linoleum cut illustrations provided by Dorothy Stewart, and the text demonstrates Kate's knowledge, artistic sense, and humor. Her goal was to point out how methods for working successfully with adobe arose out of centuries of discoveries. Some of her pronouncements are practical, others concern appropriateness, and these are mixed with some historical commentary.

Kate Chapman grappled with problems of construction and style in 1930 that are still relevant in Santa Fe in the early twenty-first century. To keep the perimeter of an adobe house dry, Kate advised continuing two old traditions. First, always slope the earth away from the exterior of an adobe house instead of placing concrete splash basins under a *canale*, the metal-lined wood scuppers that drain the roof. Second, never plant flowers at the base of the house walls. Kate promoted the monolithic strength attained by using mud plaster rather than nailing metal netting to and covering adobe walls with cement plaster because the differing rates of expansion and contraction would cause cracking. The only place she recommended impervious materials was on the roof. Kate also addressed the perennial issue that persists in adobe buildings with flat roofs, of leaks in the vicinity of the *canales*. She recommended extending the roofing felt right to the outside edge of the parapet wall, rather than tucking it in a few inches. She also pointed out how capping adobe yard walls with cement destroys the fabric below it, as the cap is undercut by rain water and melting snow.

Beyond practicalities, Kate injected her opinions about style and what was correct and what was inappropriate for adobe architecture in Santa Fe. She advised against combining features from before and after what she termed the American Occupation (1846). For example, she states that a *portal* should either have the old log posts, corbels, a heavy beam and *vigas* or milled posts, beam and wood fascia and brick coping on the parapet, but no mixture of these features. Similarly, she states that a hand-carved paneled door should not be installed in a house of the later period. In Kate's words: "Perhaps the idea is that one can quite happily add a sophisticated detail to an older structure, but not a primitive element to one of a later time." The process of adding doors or beams that are older than the current construction—to give an appearance of age—is now frowned upon by preservationists and sometimes called "earlying up" a building. Kate Chapman, unlike many people building adobe houses at the time, did *not* often insert rustic or hand-carved beams or doors from earlier buildings into her construction. When she did, it was at Margretta Dietrich's properties, and most likely at Margretta's request.

In this advice about not adding primitive elements from other buildings to current construction, Kate anticipated what decades later was codified as one of the national standards that now guide historic preservation. The Secretary of the Interior's Standards for Rehabilitation came into being when the National Historic Preservation Act passed in 1966. Standard number three states:

> Each property shall be recognized as a physical record of its time, place, and use. Changes that create a false sense of historical development, such as adding conjectural

features or architectural elements from other buildings, shall not be undertaken.

In her writing, Kate Chapman freely expressed her disdain for some new Santa Fe buildings, but not without humor. She did not shy away from dictating how New Mexico architecture should look, praising the Spanish Colonial aesthetic of simplicity in long, low buildings with few and small windows. She criticized high buildings with steps up to the entry, cellar windows, large window areas and "tacked on" porches.

One page in *Adobe Notes or How to Keep the Weather Out with Just Plain Mud* is headed Skeuomorph. The word was coined in the nineteenth century to describe the design of a new object that resembles one made in an earlier era when other materials or techniques were in use. In the new version (skeuomorph), features of the original object that are no longer functional are reproduced, thus becoming merely decorative. Kate's example is the application of only the ends of *vigas* around all sides of a building, where there are no structural *vigas* within. Another example is the occasional practice of adding superfluous bits of straw to cement plaster to give it the appearance of mud plaster. In mud plaster the straw served as a binder to inhibit shrinkage during drying; in cement plaster it represents a skeuomorph. The only sketch by Kate in all of her preserved papers occurs on a draft page of *Adobe Notes or How to Keep the Weather Out with Just Plain Mud* reproduced on the following page.

In 1966 the Spanish Colonial Arts Society, Inc. reprinted *Adobe Notes or How to Keep the Weather Out with Just Plain Mud* using the same thin colored papers and reproducing the original hand-printed effect. James Webb Young, then President of the Board of Trustees of the Laboratory of Anthropology in Santa Fe and a former advertising executive and writer, added a foreword perpetuating the image of the adobe house as illustration of ". . . centuries of practical wisdom of people who learned how to use the materials at hand, to build homes that fitted the climate and landscape in which they lived. And to give these homes forms, dimensions, and coloring, which made them a true folk art." The 1966 reprint also added short biographies of Kate Chapman, Dorothy Stewart and Spud Johnson.

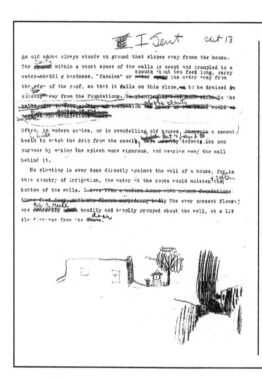

An old adobe always stands
on ground that slopes away
from the house, ℚ the earth
within a short space of the walls is swept and
trampled to a water-shedding hardness. "Canales," or spouts, about two feet long, carry the water away from the edge of the roof, so that it falls
on this slope, to be drained quickly away from
the foundations. Often, in modern copies, or in
remodelling old houses, a cement basin is built to
catch the drip from the canal, but is found to defeat its own purpose by making more vigorous the
splash that wears away the wall behind it.

No planting is ever done directly against the
wall of a house, for in this country of irrigation
the water at the roots would moisten and soften
the bottom of the walls. The ever present flowers
are, as a rule, happily and handily grouped about
the well, at a little distance from the door.

Rough draft of one page for Adobe Notes with Kate Chapman's sketch and the finished version
with linoleum block cut by Dorothy N. Stewart. Draft courtesy of School for Advanced Research
(AC02_17.1).

Adobe Notes or How to Keep the Weather Out with Just Plain Mud
was again reprinted in 1977 in its original format by agreement with the
Spanish Colonial Arts Society. It included the additional notes of the 1966
reprint, and repeated the exact format and colors of the original version.
Kate would probably have scoffed at this current 2010 reprint, losing the
color and handmade quality she desired for *Adobe Notes or How to Keep
the Weather Out with Just Plain Mud*. With apologies to Kate, the following
pages reproduce the writing, layout and linoleum-cut illustrations, if not
the original character of her work.

ADOBE NOTES

OR
HOW TO KEEP THE WEATHER OUT
WITH JUST PLAIN MUD

**Set Down in Prose & Linoleum
by KATE & D.N.S.
& Printed by SPUD**

**THE LAUGHING HORSE PRESS
TAOS, N. M. - 1930**

 HE REASON FOR MAKING PUBlic these notes, is a conviction that behind every building tradition lies an age-long series of discoveries — practical, workaday discoveries, resulting from those struggles against the forces of nature that lent zest to primitive life. Each place developed its own methods, applicable to the materials there provided by nature: stone, wood, adobe, slate or whatever, usable to keep the weather out, conserve heat, and provide a place for the preparation of food and the sheltering of children.

When the Spanish first came to New Mexico, they found a people who had been housed long enough to bring their arts to a high state of development, but not their living to a high state of comfort. Adopting the materials they found these people using, the intelligent newcomers made house making easier. They built up their adobe walls of movable, sunbaked bricks, instead of by the slow process of "puddling." They cut their roof beams, "vigas," with steel instead of stone axes. They introduced candles, and made fireplaces and bake ovens instead of merely lighting a fire in a room-corner somewhat near a hole in the roof. They made wooden doors that would open and shut. In time they learned all that could be learned about making an adobe house, and upon this slowly gathered knowledge has been built a tradition that we would do well to follow.

"The old people deed eet like that. They deen tell eet to me why they deed eet like that, but they deed eet like that."

An old adobe always stands on ground that slopes away from the house, & the earth

within a short space of the walls is swept and trampled to a water-shedding hardness. "Canales," or spouts, about two feet long, carry the water away from the edge of the roof, so that it falls on this slope, to be drained quickly away from the foundations. Often, in modern copies, or in remodelling old houses, a cement basin is built to catch the drip from the canal, but is found to defeat its own purpose by making more vigorous the splash that wears away the wall behind it.

No planting is ever done directly against the wall of a house, for in this country of irrigation the water at the roots would moisten and soften the bottom of the walls. The ever present flowers are, as a rule, happily and handily grouped about the well, at a little distance from the door.

Inertia

We advise a few hours delving in elementary physics for an understanding of Inertia, one of the strongest forces in nature, particularly in New Mexico. In this connection, nobody who was here during the War will ever forget the episode of the Army Tank and the Adobe Ruin. An old adobe house was offered by a patriotic citizen to be knocked down by the Tank. It was expected, of course, that the Tank would go through the wall at once, in a cloud of dust. The same nobody mentioned above, will forever remember the roars of laughter from the villagers, and the comic, angry sounds that came forth from the Tank, when, at the first onslaught, the great natural force called Inertia, got in its deadly work. Just plain, ordinary, old-fashioned, New Mexican Inertia, which the old-timers had counted on to keep their houses standing through the ages, and which kept this old ruin standing through the greater part of a working day, under the assaults of the Tank!

Cement capping on adobe walls, beside being excessively unattractive, is des-

tructive to the fabric beneath, for water falling on it is concentrated in a few places along the edge, channelling the wall and undercutting the cap. On the other hand, water falling on an adobe top is led gently from grain to grain, the slow displacement from above serving to fill crevices below, thickening and solidifying the base of the wall, and building up the ground level about it.

The soft, weather worn outline of pre-Spanish walls may still be seen in Santa Fe, in Manhattan Avenue at its upper end near the Acequia Madre. One of these walls is in perfect condition, standing at a right angle to the street beside a small acequia. The other is nearby, immediately on the road, and though badly eroded in former years by a shed that used to drain on it, is now ready for another three hundred years.

These walls were "puddled" in the old Indian manner, not made of movable bricks. The mud was first well "worked," a ball of convenient size being squeezed and kneaded in the hands until the air was thoroughly removed, when it was pressed into rude forms, cement-wise. Its density and toughness and water resisting qualities are extraordinary.

Permanency Removes Itself

Some people think that as adobe is ONLY MUD, and therefore soluble, it might be better to apply an outer coat of weather proof material. We are often asked if this is not a good thing to do. We reply:

This house was plastered in the eighties, with a thick coat of old style, slow-to-set lime, which had probably been slaking in a pit for a year. There is a brick coping at the top which keeps water from running between the adobe and the lime. It had only just begun to peel off around the canales in 1924, in which year the canales were made waterproof and the plaster patched. One doesn't mind patching after forty years. However, it is a good thing to remember that this type of plastered wall is well protected by the coping of brick. Where this protection is lacking, as, for instance, where plaster is run up over a firewall to imitate adobe, the life of the plaster is shorter.

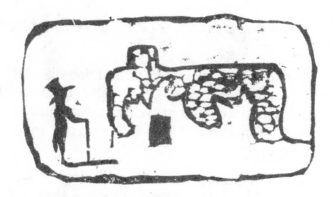

This house, "permanently" plastered in 1927,
speaks for itself.

Re-plastering an adobe house with adobe
means, simply, taking from the dooryard the dirt
that has washed down from the walls, and put-
ting it back on top of the walls again, every third
year. The weather-proof plaster, with good luck,
will last between twelve and fifteen years. It has
been calculated that the initial cost of the water
proof plastering, capitalized, would produce e-
nough income to keep an adobe wall in repair.

During the early days of the American Occupation, owing to the number of well trained car-
penters and good saw mills, larger windows with
sliding sash began to be used, and conventionally
panelled doors appeared. The Italian stone cutters
brought over by Archbishop Lamy to work on the
Cathedral, are given the credit for introducing the
brick cornice above lime plastered walls. This style
calls for the portal with the graceful, tapered,
square pillars and boxed-in viga ends, the box running the length of the portal, on the outside, and
overhanging by six or eight inches the beam that
supports the vigas. The vigas show in the ceiling
of the portal, but cannot be seen from the outside.
We have never seen an old house of the brick pretil type with exposed viga ends.

Whether a house is of the earliest and most
primitive, the middle, or the latest and most sophisticated period, there is a general rule that was
never broken, and that contributes to the restful-
ness of the Santa Fe "effect": the portal is either
inset, with rooms on three sides of it, or it must
cover the entire length of the house, or the length
and one side, or the two sides of an L, or the four
sides of a patio; but it is never tacked on the
house around the front door, like a porch or stoop.

Adobe laid up in adobe is best, for it becomes in time one solid mass. For instance, a keystone of brick or stone acts as a unit pressing against other units. In adobe, the keystone becomes a part of the whole mass, as proven by the fact that a crack in an adobe arch is not stepped down between the adobe bricks, but runs through it as it would do in concrete. Therefore a cracked adobe wall or a cracked arch, will stand for many years if not subjected to constant jarring. On the other hand, the constant rise and fall in the wind of a pitched roof has been known to crumble to powder the adobe wall supporting it, at all the points where the uprights rested.

Temperature changes expand and contract different materials at different rates, hence "reinforcing" adobe with nails or wire or cement, breaks up its one-ness.

The uneven or hand-made surface of indoor walls, so much admired, is best produced as the old-timers produced it—by the use of a smallish, primitive trowel, wielded by a not-too-expert hand, with entire lack of mechanical guide. Even the most accomplished workman, thus equipped, will be unable to plaster with too great a degree of regularity.

To the earliest Spanish period, belong the delightfully carved and panelled doors

and shutters now so much seen in Antique shops, and also the round-posted portal, or long porch, with or without corbels. This kind of portal always had an adobe pretil, or cornice, never a brick one; whereas the squared and tapered post was always coped with brick, never with adobe.

This is an important point, and we wish people would consider it more carefully. The "mixed" buildings of Europe that we find so charming, were mixed in a consistent manner. A Gothic Cathedral might be built over a Norman crypt, a house might take on a Tudor wing, but each style was allowed its own character. Nobody ever attempted to fit a bit of Tudor panelling about a Gothic window; while the Norman crypt remains a Norman crypt today.

We do not like to see an "early" portal on a house of later style, nor carved and hand-panelled doors where the Early-American-Occupation mill work is more suitable.

Perhaps the idea is that one can quite happily add a sophisticated detail to an older structure, but not a primitive element to one of a later time.

THE FIRST THING to do when remodelling an old place is to put on a waterproof
roof. Of course none of the old houses were covered with any material beside graded dirt, which
carries the water off in ordinary weather, snow
being removed before it has a chance to soak in;
slow, soft rains are the very worst sort for an a-
dobe roof, as they saturate the surface thoroughly, but fortunately they are fairly rare in this region, and the short, heavy rains run off before
much damage is done..

We sometimes hear people say that their
roofs leaked around the edge, so that it was necessary to put on a brick or cement coping. Leaks
of this sort are almost always the result of skimped
flashing. The "built up" felt and asphalt should
reach right to the outer edge of the firewall, then
a single line of adobe bricks should be laid upon
this, topped by a "cavallete" or rounded crown of
mud. This crown can be saturated with water,
can be almost washed off till there is only enough
left to keep the roof-edges from blowing away in
the wind, and still not leak. BUT, if the flashing
has been just tucked in an inch or two, only an
inch or two can wear away without disaster.

Often when geography required draining an
old house to the north, the roof was made to overhang along that side. Old timers explain that the
mass of ice on the shaded end of the
canal forms a dam which backs up
the water to the very portion of the
roof which is least protected. By using vigas a few feet longer, and laying the roof on them so that it projects several feet beyond the outer
edge of the wall, the lowest area,
with its almost inevitable leak, hangs
harmlessly over empty space.

Of the purely fake Santa Fe house, the slightly disguised bungalow on a suburban grass plat, set off by cement walks, there is no need to speak in this book. Those who like one sort don't like the other. But we are irresistibly impelled to refer to one other, perhaps even more irritating type—the HIGH HOUSE.

The HIGH HOUSE stands about eight feet higher than a proper adobe should, because its builder has missed the whole spirit and flavour of the Architecture of this region. An adobe house should be low and long and close to the earth.

The HIGH HOUSE has a firewall that towers above the vigas, structurally needless, but probably intended to be imposing. Its front door is approached by a flight of steps instead of by a gentle grade, because the house floors are several feet above the ground level.

At the rear, where sloping ground has made excavation economical, there is a cellar (though who would choose to run up and down cellar steps

at this altitude?) and an insistently noticeable
row of ugly cellar windows. We are not supposed
to see these, though nothing has been done to con-
ceal them. They are behind the house, therefore,
to the polite, invisible. But we are not polite. We
view them with regretful emotion, perhaps even
a slight shyness, a bit reminiscent of the admix-
ture of pain and amusement with which we viewed
the Hamburg ruffles showing beneath the white
skirts of the little girl who joined the May Procession a trifle late, frantically clutching her hip, and
muttering:

 "Por Dios, I knew I'd forget something!"

Because the housewife who has a dirt floor, literally does "sweep out" her house every day, and because the outside ground level is constantly being built up by the wash from roof and wall, an old house usually has a low floor level, frequently eight inches deeper than the doorsill, as have the houses in Palestine and presumably in all other places where dirt floors are the rule. People who have allowed this quaint feature to remain in their "done over" houses, by laying floors at the low level, have found their rooms free from floor-draft and therefore easy to heat. Floors are never damp in this dry climate — provided, of course, that roof water and acequias are properly handled. In several old houses we have found heavy joists that have lain directly on the dirt for forty years, as fresh and unrotted as if they had been put in last month.

The windows of the oldest houses are few and quite small, and the doors low, so that heat is kept in during Winter, and out in Summer. All the light that enters is used by reflection from the white walls, and none lost by absorption. In a room with long, unbroken wall space, the absence of glare is a rest and relief from the power and brightness of our much boasted sun. The huge areas of glass of the American manner, which originated in cloudy climates, necessitate colouring the inside walls to absorb light and prevent eyestrain, a double departure from the true type.

Old timers never made an opening in a wall very close to a corner, a safe rule being that the space between an opening and the outside corner is always wider than the opening itself. The solidity of the corner is thus assured, and our old standby, Inertia, does the rest.

The great old Hacienda had no "rear," for the service part of the establishment was close to the chicken yard and goat corral, where left overs were so readily consumed as to do away with the need of garbage collection. The smaller house was equally rearless, the chickens roaming at will, the goats near at hand, each of the numerous doors tidy and inviting, with the "Big Front Door" distinguishable only by its superior gaiety of color. The average American copy of a Santa Fe house, even when perfect in other respects, is almost certain to proclaim itself by a regrettable back porch of wood and screening, standing high on stilts, and flanked by wood piles and coal boxes and refuse tins.

This paragraph, we hope, will be taken as a plea for the service court, much used in other places, but here, all too rare. We consider it one of Modernity's most admirable contributions to domestic Architecture.

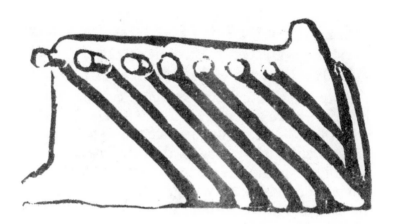

In the old, far-off days before the Spanish
people came, Indians cut their vigas with stone
axes, and, having no beasts of burden, brought
them from the forest by lashing each viga across
three or four carrying-poles, each of these held by
two men. There is a tradition that the immense
timbers for the Acoma church were first blessed
as living trees where they stood, then brought
in this manner, without ever touching the ground,
from the slopes of San Mateo, twenty-five miles
away.

The Spanish builders cut their vigas with
steel axes, and made a hole in the thicker end,
through which the thongs of an ox yoke were passed, the smaller end dragging on the ground and
wearing itself to a point. Vigas of this sort are
still to be seen in many houses in Santa Fe.

Spanish and Indian builder alike, on reaching
the house-site, laid the vigas across the walls with
the excess length left to take care fo itself by pro-
truding from the outer wall. There was no reason
for this except the very simple and utilitarian one
of letting well enough alone: for who would both-
er to spend hours and hours cutting off the ends

with a stone hatchet; or who, later, would dull the edge of a precious tool, when nothing was to be gained by it? Thus developed a fortuitous feature that sets apart the New Mexican house in the eyes of the visitor: for what is lovelier than viga shadows slanting along the weathered surface of an adobe wall?

Skeuomorph

An enthusiastic admirer of the Santa Fe Style once called projecting viga ends "intriguing in their honesty," then trotted off to introduce the style to her home town. As this town lies in the midst of a completely treeless region, beams strong enough to support a roof are prohibitive in cost, so two-foot stubs, touchingly "intriguing" in their *dis*honesty, were shipped in and tacked in rows along the outside, for effect. In time the builders, a bit over-inventive, began to arrange them one above another, then in necklace patterns, then in diamond shapes; as significant, structurally, as raisins on a cake.

So the viga fashion spread, till a builder in our own town, bent on producing a building of the heaped up, pressed down, running over, extra special Santa Fe variety, has brought the pathetic viga-stubs home to roost in a neat, level band, not on just two, but on all four sides of his tower—perhaps "intriguing," perhaps not—but at all events unhampered by honesty.

MUST we say anything about bell-less bel-
fries? Or humps along the sky-line? Let's **not!**

The outstanding quality of the Architecture of this region is simplicity. The earth, poor or rich, makes the walls, the forest trees the ceilings; so that the house of the Pueblo and the house of the Millionaire are not so very different. It is the only place in the world where this is so. Many people who could easily afford the exoticism of red tiles and plaster, lovely in other adobe countries, have with commendable restraint decided against them in favor of the homely "mud" of the land. In this lies Santa Fe's distinction. There is a feeling almost of apology for any appearance of prosperity too great to be in harmony with the surrounding bad lands, never far away, encircling each little fertile valley where the "gente", close to the earth and unhampered by many possessions, still wrest a living from great space and little water. There life goes on enriched by a sense of beauty and an inate dignity that are left over from an older time, when hard work and infinite care, not money, were spent to beautify a house and its furnishings.

5

Kate's House in the Hills

In 1933 Kate Chapman began plans to build a new home for her family. Kate's friend and associate Dorothy Stewart and the Chapmans had each purchased land in the foothills east of town. Dorothy planned a studio and Kate a house. The north boundary of the land Kate bought from Emiterio and Antonia G. Ribera coincided with about 1500 feet of Arroyo de las Moras (now called Arroyo Mora).[1] The National Forest was adjacent to the property, and the land contained steeply sloping hills offering excellent views to the west. Kate and Dorothy selected two of the more gently sloping areas with relatively level building sites for their structures.

The L-shaped house Kate designed at this site was the closest she ever came to using the features of the Santa Fe Style. Still, she displayed her usual originality in departing from the large *viga*s and *latillas*, or small poles, above them. Instead, she placed medium-sized logs immediately next to each other in one ceiling. Therefore, a continuous row of ends of the roof structure poles project through the adobe walls instead of the usual widely spaced *viga* ends. This type of roof appeared occasionally in historic Santa Fe buildings, but did not become a feature of the revival style.

The Chapman house in the foothills included an adobe horno and a fenced garden.
Photograph Courtesy of Museum of New Mexico (#028124).

The mud-plastered corner of the Chapman house, the horno, and an outbuilding.
Photograph Courtesy of Peggy Harnisch.

The ends of the ceiling structure logs at the Chapman house extend, creating an overhang. Photograph Courtesy of Peggy Harnisch.

Kate might have gone on to design and build more houses had she not unexpectedly died at the age of fifty-eight from complications after an emergency appendectomy. In 1944, soon after Kate's death, Dorothy Stewart wrote a letter to her own heirs stating her preference for the eventual distribution of certain of her possessions. At that time, Dorothy wanted her studio on two acres in the foothills to be given to Maria Chabot, along with rights to the spring water, given that the Chapman house had first priority. Stewart described her studio as directly across the Arroyo de las Moras from the Chapman house and also referred to the "Chapman Stewart Road."[2] Chabot was a journalist whom Kate, Dorothy and Margretta had met during one of their trips to Mexico. Dietrich hired Chabot as her assistant when she served as President of the New Mexico Association on Indian Affairs (NMAIA).

In the early 1950s, both the Chapman's house and Dorothy's studio nearby were vandalized. After Kate's death, Kenneth Chapman had given up trying to maintain the vacant building. In Irene Von Horvath's words: he watched its gradual destruction, including stolen windows, doors, roofing and *vigas*.[3] The Chapman's granddaughter Peggy Harnisch relates a story about how Kenneth Chapman very literally "watched its gradual destruction." On one of his trips up to check on the house when he was in his eighties, Kenneth and his brother Dwight came upon two vandals carrying away a door from the house. The brothers, both over eighty years old, stepped behind a juniper tree. When the thieves neared it, they jumped out, exclaiming, "Boo!" The thieves dropped the door and fled.[4] Kenneth Chapman eventually authorized the complete removal of the last house Kate designed and built.

6

Kate Chapman in Perspective

To appreciate Kate Chapman's role in Santa Fe history and to place her in a broader perspective, this final chapter shifts attention beyond her work in historic preservation and architecture. Reference to Kate's milieu, to the architecture in Santa Fe at the time, and some description of her other activities will round out the picture of her multifaceted contributions to Santa Fe. The account of these additional pursuits also hints at her lively, irreverent personality.

In the early twentieth century, artists, writers and many well educated, independent women with a rebellious spirit were attracted to Northern New Mexico from places as diverse as Chicago, Boston, Wisconsin and California, as well as Philadelphia. Whether settling in Santa Fe or quieter places north of it, these women rejected the stilted atmosphere of their homes and the restrictions of their culture. Amidst the Southwestern landscapes, arts, and cultures, they felt a freedom denied them in the places they fled. A network of nonconformist women formed, and occasionally joined with the other groups of recent newcomers: those who had come to New Mexico hoping to cure their pulmonary illnesses, the artists, and the archaeologists associated with the Museum of New Mexico and School of American Archaeology.[1] Together, they formed an active intelligentsia who not only valued, but worked in support of, the Native cultures of New Mexico. Kate Chapman seems to have been equally at ease among the unorthodox, spontaneous artists, the more academic archaeologists, and the activist women.

Viewed as outrageous by her husband's conservative relatives in Chicago, Kate was free spirited and sociable. She had friends that ranged from Santa Fe to the pueblos. Among the newcomers from Philadelphia in the late 1920s were some friends of Margretta Dietrich and Dorothy Stewart. Setting out on a family trip west in 1929, Martha and William Field planned to meet their daughter Lois and her daughter Marcia in Santa Fe. The Fields soon settled in Santa Fe, becoming active supporters of the Spanish Colonial Arts Society founded in 1925 by writer Mary Austin and artist Frank Applegate. During 1929 Lois Field kept a diary, in which she recorded how fortunate she felt to have Mrs. Chapman as a guide to the area. Field wrote that Mrs. Chapman ". . . knows every stone and piñon tree, not to mention every inhabitant."[2] A friend of Kate's was dancing at Santo Domingo Pueblo the day Lois Field visited. Field was amazed that not only the dancer's daughter, but everyone else called Mrs. Chapman "Kate," regardless of their age.[3]

It was common in the 1920s for the newly arrived artists without formal architectural background to design and build their own adobe houses, but it was rare for a woman. Many of the male artists had either experience building houses or had taken a class or two related to architecture; Kate had neither. One of the male artists went far beyond building a home for his own family, and began designing houses and even public buildings for clients. William Penhallow Henderson had experience with the construction of his own house in Illinois before moving to Santa Fe and had some training in engineering. He started a design and construction business in Santa Fe in 1925. Henderson and his partners John Evans and Edwin Brooks opened the Pueblo Spanish Building Company, and produced hand-carved wood furniture, as well as buildings. The compound Henderson designed for former New Yorkers, Amelia and Martha White, later became the School for American Research and the School for Advanced Research (SAR). The company instituted by Henderson, Evans and Brooks designed major additions to Sena Plaza, as well as the Museum of Navajo Ceremonial Art, now known as the Wheelwright Museum of the American Indian. Artist Frank Applegate had taken an architectural modeling class in college and had built a home in Pennsylvania before his arrival in Santa Fe.[4] He designed several houses and major additions to the preexisting De La Peña house. The architectural work of such artists is better known than that of Kate Chapman, and hers preceded them by several years.

In the early decades of the twentieth century, throughout New Mexico there were few professional architects in private practice. The first architects had only arrived in New Mexico after the railway brought the new building materials suitable for the "American" style buildings. "Whereas buildings had previously been either simple enough structurally or stylistically as not to warrant the services of a professionally trained specialist, the styles and complexities of post railroad buildings soon began to demand them."[5] Architects, in addition to working in the "imported" styles began to design public buildings in the new Spanish Pueblo Revival Style. By 1920, architect Isaac Hamilton Rapp had designed several public buildings, including the Gross Kelly Warehouse in 1914 and The Museum of Fine Arts in 1915, but closed his Santa Fe office in 1921. At the time Kate first began her buildings at Plaza Balentine, Rapp had left Santa Fe, and John Gaw Meem was in Denver apprenticing in the architectural office of Fisher and Fisher.

Though Kate ventured into a field infrequently occupied by women throughout the Southwest, the well-known Mary Jane Colter preceded her by twenty years. Colter accomplished her first architectural design in Arizona in 1905, and the path leading to Colter's career in architecture included an apprenticeship in an architect's office in San Francisco. The year Kate arrived in Santa Fe, Colter designed the interior of Louis Curtiss' El Ortiz Hotel in Lamy, New Mexico. In the whole state of New Mexico, only a sprinkling of women were working in architecture in the 1920s. Two examples were Kate Nichols Chavez in Albuquerque and Lillie B. Lamar in Santa Rosa, New Mexico.[6] In Santa Fe Katherine Stinson Otero stepped into the field of adobe architecture about eight years after Kate Chapman began her work. One Santa Fe resident in the 1920s, Alice Clark Myers, was the first female graduate in architecture from the Chicago Art Institute, but did not pursue a career as architect.

In addition to contributing her adobe work, Kate Chapman played a role in three pivotal events of Santa Fe history in the early twentieth century. Kate played a part in the development of festivities surrounding Zozobra in 1919, the defeat of the Bursum Bill in Congress in 1922, and the squelching of a Santa Fe "culture center" proposed by the a branch of the Federation of Women's Clubs in 1926. Kate Chapman's activism is known even less than her role as adobe expert and builder.

While artist Will Shuster is called the "father of Zozobra," in fact, several people were involved in the origin of the giant puppet representing gloom during Santa Fe's annual Fiesta. Shuster fabricated the first body and was involved with Zozobra for four decades, but Gustave Baumann made the first head, and newspaper editor Dana Johnson contributed the name. However, long before construction began, the Zozobra phenomenon started with the effort of Kate Chapman and Dorothy Stewart to "revive an affair similar to the Mummers Parade" that they knew in their native Philadelphia. In the Philadelphia event, which continues today, Kate and Dorothy remembered people carrying a figure of a gloomy one or wicked soul while a lot of others with colorful whips were whipping the effigy during a New Year's parade. According to Shuster, "Out of this hatched the idea of making an Old Man Gloom."[7] The first figure was about 18 feet high, and resembled the traditional figure of Philadelphia. There were a group of artists dressed up as the "merrymakers" who whipped the "glooms," people dressed in black walking in procession around Zozobra. After that first year, the festivities began to take on the characteristics familiar today.

In a more serious realm, Kate Chapman also joined with other newcomers to Santa Fe promoting Indian welfare and Indian art in the 1920s and 1930s. Kate and her husband Kenneth both became members of the newly formed New Mexico Association on Indian Affairs (NMAIA) soon after Alice Corbin Henderson, Elizabeth Sergeant, Mary Austin and Mabel Dodge Lujan founded the organization in 1922.[8] The catalyst for formation of the group was the need to publicize the violation of Pueblo Indians' rights being threatened in a new bill proposed in Congress in 1922. The Republican Senator from New Mexico, Holm O. Bursum, introduced the bill in an attempt to settle claims of non-Indian residents on Pueblo lands because in many cases boundaries of grants issued by first the Spanish, and then Mexico, and finally the U.S. overlapped. The legislation sought to settle land disputes between the Pueblo Indians and non-Indians who had settled after 1848 on land within the boundaries of the Pueblo land grants. The bill's introduction provoked clamor on behalf of the New Mexico Pueblo people's rights to keep the land they were granted by the Spanish in the seventeenth and eighteenth centuries. Many saw it as a threat to Indian cultural survival. Kate's friend Margaret McKittrick led the local protest and served as the chair of the new organization. The All Pueblo Council took their case to Washington, and within a year the Bursum Pueblo Land Bill was defeated.[9]

Kate Chapman and Dorothy Stewart's behind-the-scenes actions affected another turning point later in 1920s Santa Fe. This time they had a role in preventing a large development in the foothills east of town, though the objection was based on differences of opinion about the meaning of "culture," not on development per se. Representatives of the Federated Women's Clubs of nine states of the South and Midwest primarily from Texas came to Santa Fe in 1926 to request that the city donate land for their proposed chatauqua or "cultural colony." By then, interest in chatauquas was declining across the country after peaking in 1924. Named for the original location of a Methodist summer retreat founded in 1874 in New York State, chatauquas brought a summer program of music, lectures and poetry reading, and were usually held in tents. However, the center proposed for Santa Fe was to include an auditorium and some permanent summerhouses in a "vacation and educational atmosphere."[10]

The land that the City Council selected was in the foothills east of town near Sunmount Sanatorium. Opposition to the proposal became loud and fierce, directed principally by writer Mary Austin, among many others. In Austin's view, the "chatauqua" had connotations of status seeking, pretentiousness and provinciality. Austin voiced her opinion that chatauqua-minded "invaders" lacking their own culture would threaten the authentic culture of Santa Fe. Austin proclaimed that there are ". . . two types of cultural centre, the creative and the chatauqua, and the two are incompatible in the same community. Having one, we prefer not to have the other. . . ."[11]

The group of protestors saw themselves as protecting the original cultures of the area and perhaps as being "above" the group of people proposing the colony in Santa Fe. Margretta Dietrich wrote in her memoirs,

"But while the intelligentsia of Santa Fe was opposing the bringing of 'culture,' Dorothy Stewart and Kate Chapman quietly bought up all the pieces of land which were to be included in the site."[12] Santa Fe County deed records confirm that, beginning in 1926, Kate Chapman and Dorothy Stewart purchased several parcels of land in the foothills. The threat of the chatauqua also spurred a protest meeting to be held at the Sunmount Sanatorium, and that meeting led to the formation of the Old Santa Fe Association. Therefore, more than a decade after Kate's involvement in the promotion of the new Santa Fe Style at the museum, she was present at the formation of an organization that continues to focus on preserving Santa Fe architecture.

Kate Chapman was considered proficient enough to be listed among thirty writers living in Santa Fe in a visitor's guide to Santa Fe printed in 1931.[13] Besides *Adobe Notes, or How to Keep the Rain out with Just Plain Mud*, Kate's other writing projects included several short stories and about twenty poems. Drawings or records pertaining to her adobe work—if she had them—did not survive, but drafts of her writings did. With the poems that survive in her papers is a note saying she was sending three of her poems to the *Christian Science Monitor* or the *Atlantic*, and couldn't decide which. One poem entitled "Old Love" was printed in 1938 in The New Mexico Sentinel's New Mexico Writers section edited by Haniel Long, whose associates in the venture were Witter Bynner, Erna Fergusson, Paul Horgan and Frieda Lawrence. Of all of Kate's writing, her missive about adobe remains the most important.

In terms of adobe architecture, Kate's primary legacy remains in her sensitive work on important historic properties, such as the Juan José Prada House, El Zaguan and the Borrego House. The projects illustrating her originality and capacity for strong design of new houses have been so altered that only her black and white photographs remain as testimony to Kate's potential as a designer. Adobe eventually went from being the material that was readily at hand to the most expensive one for building. Of course, buildings in Santa Fe now often employ a wide variety of materials and techniques, all with the intent of appearing to be constructed of adobe. Kate Chapman understood the value of using traditional materials and methods in building true adobe houses in Santa Fe. The respect she so strongly felt for the local historic building traditions did not come from idle nostalgia, but from her firsthand experience with local people and their building methods.

Kate Chapman's contributions to Santa Fe history lasted only a few decades after her arrival in 1910. Kate's efforts in archaeology, poetry, and in the cultural life of the city are virtually unknown, and her drawing skills are only suggested by her art school years and her work documenting art in the Pajarito Plateau cave dwellings for the Museum of New Mexico. She did not label the photographs of her projects in her two albums, and the prize-winning builder and writer is identified as "housewife" in the census of 1930. On the cover of *Adobe Notes or How to Keep the Weather Out with Just Plain Mud*, the last names of Dorothy Stewart, Spud Johnson, or Kate Chapman do not appear. The cryptic anonymity of "Kate, D.N.S. and Spud" perhaps symbolizes Kate's consistent pattern of accomplishing a lot and promoting herself little. Kate Chapman relished life and challenged current mores. She wore jodhpurs and explored the Southwest in the kind of contraption that several Santa Fe artists, in this case Dorothy Stewart, improvised for travel. Through a multitude of outlets, Kate Chapman expressed both her humor and her serious concerns, leaving a lasting imprint on Santa Fe.

Kate Chapman in 1936 standing in front of Dorothy Stewart's truck, with the dog, Fanny. Photograph Courtesy of School for Advanced Research (AC02_743.26a).

Notes

Chapter 1

1. Rosemary Nusbaum, *The City Different and The Palace*. Santa Fe: Sunstone Press, 1978, 89-90.
2. Janet Chapman and Karen Barrie. *Kenneth Milton Chapman, A Life Dedicated to Indian Arts and Artists*. Albuquerque: University of New Mexico Press, 2008, 72.
3. Bainbridge Bunting, *John Gaw Meem, Southwestern Architect*. Albuquerque: University of New Mexico Press, 1983, 7. Bunting also named Kenneth Chapman, attorney Frank Springer, editor of *The New Mexican* A.F. Walter, merchant Dan Kelly, architect Isaac Hamilton Rapp, and Dr. Frank Mera of Sunmount Sanitarium.
4. Nusbaum, *The City Different and The Palace*, 80.
5. Carlos Vierra, "New Mexico Architecture." *Art and Archaeology*, Vol. VII. Nos.1-2 January-February. (Washington, DC, The Archaeological Institute of America 1918), 37-49.
6. Nusbaum, *The City Different and The Palace*, 87.
7. Carl D. Sheppard, *Creator of the Santa Fe Style, Isaac Hamilton Rapp*. Albuquerque: University of New Mexico Press, 1988, 77.
8. Ibid, 59.
9. Marit K. Munson, editor, *Kenneth Chapman's Santa Fe, Artists and Archaeologists, 1907–1931, The Memoirs of Kenneth Chapman*. Santa Fe: New Mexico School for Advanced Research Press, 2007, 61.
10. Chris Wilson, *The Myth of Santa Fe, Creating a Modern Regional Tradition*. Albuquerque: University of New Mexico Press, 2003, 127.
11. Janet Chapman and Karen Barrie, 116.
12. SAR photo AC 02 818b, hand written note on back of photo.
13. Interview with Steve Hughes, who grew up at Plaza Balentine, April 29, 2008.

Chapter 2

1. United States Federal Census 1880 and 1910.

Chapter 3

1. Nabokov, Peter and Robert Easton, *Native American Architecture*. Oxford: Oxford University Press, 1989, 366.

2. The Baumann house on Camino de Las Animas, the Cutting house on Old Santa Fe Trail and the Wilson house on East Buena Vista Street each have remnants of this fence type.

3. Thomas, Trent, Historic American Building Survey Report, 1.

4. *Premios Ganados Por Las Casas Tipicas, El Pasatiempo*, Santa Fe New Mexican, August 30, 1934, 1.

Chapter 5

1. Warranty Deed, Santa Fe County Records.

2. Dorothy N. Stewart, Letter to Heirs, 1944 with notes of 1954.

3. Irene Von Horvath, "The Dorothy N. Stewart Trail," 2000, 1.

4. Peggy Harnisch Interview, February 1, 2010.

Chapter 6

1. The School of American Archaeology was renamed the School of American Research in 1917. The name was changed to School for Advanced Research in 2007.

2. Lois Field, "Diary." 21.

3. Ibid, 27.

4. Labinsky, Daria & Stan Hieronymus. *Frank Applegate of Santa Fe, Artist & Preservationist*. Albuquerque: LPD Press, p.62.

5. Boyd Pratt, "Directory of Historic New Mexico Architects," unpublished, xiv.

6. Boyd Pratt, "A Brief History of the Practice of Architecture in New Mexico," New Mexico Architecture, November/December 1989, 9.

7. "Oral history interview with Will Shuster," 1964 July 30, Archives of American Art, Smithsonian Institution. Historic Santa Fe Foundation Files.

8. Janet Chapman and Karen Barrie. *Kenneth Milton Chapman, A Life Dedicated to Indian Arts and Artists*. Albuquerque: University of New Mexico Press, 2008, 177.

9. Margaret McKittrick, *Bulletin of New Mexico Association on Indian Affairs*, "The Pueblo Land Problem," 6.

10. Molly Mullin, *Culture in the Marketplace*, 101-2.

11. Marta Weigle and Kyle Fiore, *Santa Fe & Taos the Writer's Era, 1916–1941*, New Edition. Santa Fe: Sunstone Press, 2008, 21.

12. Margretta Dietrich, "New Mexico Recollections, Part II," 14.

13. Marta Weigle and Kyle Fiore, *Santa Fe & Taos: The Writer's Era, 1916–1941*, New Edition. Santa Fe: Sunstone Press, 2008, 36.

List of Projects

T he list of projects contains the location and the type of property use of each in 2012. Note that Kate Chapman worked on other houses in the vicinity of Acequia Madre and Delgado Street, and perhaps future research will reveal more detailed information about them.

1. Plaza Balentine houses are on a private lane off of Acequia Madre east of Delgado Street. They are each private residential properties.

2. The compound behind El Zaguan (James L. Johnson House) on Canyon Road contains private residential properties plus the Historic Santa Fe Foundation landscape and outbuildings.

3. Chapman House 2 that was formerly on Camino Cruz Blanca has been demolished.

4. The east side of the Arthur Boyle House at 327 De Vargas Street is part of a private residence.

5. The Chapman House 1 is at 615 Acequia Madre, and is a private residential property.

6. El Zaguan, also known as the James L. Johnson House at 545 Canyon Road, contains the office of the Historic Santa Fe Foundation as well as private apartments. The garden and west end of the building are open to the public during foundation office hours.

7. The Garcia-Stevenson House is at 408 Delgado Street, and is privately owned.

8. The Delgado-Hare House is at 401 Delgado Street, and is a private residence.

9. The Juan José Prada House, which became Margretta Dietrich's home, is located at 519 Canyon Road. It is a private home with a greatly altered landscape.

10. The Borrego House at 724 Canyon Road has been the location of successive restaurants for decades.

Bibliography

Published Material

Bunting, Bainbridge. *John Gaw Meem, Southwestern Architect.* Albuquerque: University of New Mexico Press, 1983.

Chapman, Janet and Karen Barrie. *Kenneth Milton Chapman, A Life Dedicated to Indian Arts and Artists.* Albuquerque: University of New Mexico Press, 2008.

Chauvenet, Beatrice. *Hewett and Friends, A Biography of Santa Fe's Vibrant Era.* Santa Fe: Museum of New Mexico Press, 1983.

Grattan, Virginia L. *Mary Colter, Builder Upon the Red Earth.* Flagstaff: Northland Press, 1980.

Labinsky, Daria and Stan Hieronymus. *Frank Applegate of Santa Fe: Artist and Preservationist.* Albuquerque: LPD Press, 2001.

Mullin, Molly H. *Culture in the Marketplace, Gender, Art, and Value in the American Southwest.* Durham and London: Duke University Press, 2001.

Munson, Marit K. editor. *Kenneth Chapman's Santa Fe, Artists and Archaeologists, 1907–1931, The Memoirs of Kenneth Chapman.* Santa Fe: School for Advanced Research Press, 2007.

Nabokov, Peter and Robert Easton, *Native American Architecture.* Oxford: Oxford University Press, 1989.

Nusbaum, Rosemary. *The City Different and The Palace.* Santa Fe: Sunstone Press, 1978.

Pratt, Boyd C. "A Brief History of the Practice of Architecture in New Mexico." *New Mexico Architecture,* November/December 1989: 8-15.

Sheppard, Carl D. *Creator of the Santa Fe Style, Isaac Hamilton Rapp, Architect.* Albuquerque: University of New Mexico Press, 1988.

Tobias, Henry J. and Charles E. Woodhouse. *Santa Fe, A Modern History 1880–1990.* Albuquerque: University of New Mexico Press, 2001.

Vierra, Carlos. "New Mexico Architecture." *Art and Archaeology,* Vol.VII. Nos.1-2, January-February (1918) 37-49.

Weigle, Marta and Kyle Fiore. *Santa Fe & Taos the Writer's Era, 1916–1941.* New Edition. Santa Fe: Sunstone Press, 2008.

Wilson, Chris. *The Myth of Santa Fe, Creating a Modern Regional Tradition.* Albuquerque: University of New Mexico Press, 2003.

Unpublished Documents

Dietrich, Margretta Stewart. "New Mexico Recollections Parts I and II." Santa Fe: Vergara Printing Company 1959, 1961 (Historic Santa Fe Foundation).

Sze, Corinne P., PhD. "El Zaguan, The James L. Johnson House, 545 Canyon Road, A Social History," 1997 (Historic Santa Fe Foundation).

———. "The Field House, Las Milpas. 2 Cerro Gordo Road, Santa Fe New Mexico, A History of the Property." October 1, 1991 (Historic Santa Fe Foundation).

Ericson, Lief and Herbert E. Mueller. "A History of The Borrego House, 724 Canyon Road, Santa Fe, New Mexico 1753–1946" (Old Santa Fe Association).

McKittrick, Margaret. "The Pueblo Land Problem." (Foreword to the New Mexico Association on Indian Affairs Bulletin, Mudd Manuscript Library, Princeton University.)

Stewart, Dorothy N. Letter to Heirs, 1944 with notes of 1954 (Historic Santa Fe Foundation).

Trent, Thomas. *The Borrego House*, Historic American Buildings Survey No. N.M.-14. 1940. 1940 Public Works Administration Program Federal Project 498 A, April 10, 1940. Drawings Delineated by R. P. McClung.

El Pasatiempo, Aug 30, 1930, "Prize-winning houses in Santa Fe Architectural Competitions."

Field, Lois. "Diary from 1927 to 1930," courtesy Bill Field, Spanish Colonial Arts Society.

Loomis, Sylvia. "Interview of Will Shuster," July 30, 1964, for the Archives of American Art, Smithsonian Institute (Historic Santa Fe Foundation).

Pratt, Boyd C. With Carleen Lazzell and Chris Wilson, "Draft Directory of Historic New Mexico Architects," 1988 (Zimmerman Library Center For Southwest Research).

Von Horvath, Irene. "The Dorothy N. Stewart Trail" (Historic Santa Fe Foundation).

Index

CPSIA information can be obtained
at www.ICGtesting.com
Printed in the USA
BVHW070247280620
582383BV00005B/955